I DREAM MYSELF INTO BEING

I DREAM MYSELF INTO BEING

COLLECTED POEMS

JOHN THOMPSON

Anansi

Copyright © 1991 by Shirley Gibson

All rights reserved. No part of this publication may be reproduced or transmitted in any form, or by any means, electronic or mechanical, including photocopy, recording or any information storage or retrieval system, without permission in writing from the publisher.

Published in 1991 by
House of Anansi Press Limited
1800 Steeles Avenue West
Concord, Ontario
L4K 2P3

Publishing History

Part I, "At the Edge of the Chopping There Are No Secrets," first published in book form by House of Anansi Press Limited in 1973.

Part II, "Stilt Jack," first published in book form by House of Anansi Press Limited in 1978.

Canadian Cataloguing in Publication Data
Thompson, John, 1938-1976
I dream myself into being

ISBN 0-88784-507-X

I. Title

PS8589.H5912 1991   C811' .54   C91-093424-X
PR9199.3.T5612 1991

Cover Design: Brant Cowie / ArtPlus Limited
Page Make-Up: Denise Danford / ArtPlus Limited

Printed in Canada

CONTENTS

Introduction / Remembering John Thompson
by James Polk / 1

I / At the Edge of the Chopping There Are No Secrets

Wife / 13
Household / 14
Partridge / 15
Our Arcs Touch / 16
Apple Tree / 17
Horse Chestnuts / 18
Fish / 19
Horse / 20
Barn / 21
Scene / 22
Black Smith Shop / 23
Turnip Field / 24
After the Rain / 25
Colville's Crow / 26
Crow and Rabbit / 27
Crow's Wing / 28
The Image / 29
First Day of Winter / 30
Zero / 31
Cold Wind / 32
The Great Bear / 33
January February March Et Cetera / 34
The Supermarket Invaded / 35
Dung Day / 36
What Are You Asking For? / 37
Return / 38

"Winter Is By Far the Oldest Season" / 39
The Skins of a Dream / 41
Down Below / 42
The Narrow Road / 43
Moving Out, Moving In / 44
Burnt Coat Head / 46
Picasso: *La Jeune Fille Sur La boule;*
Lascaux: *Stag Frieze* / 48
Norman Towers / 49
On the Tolar Canal / 50
The Change / 51
Ewe's Skull on the Aboideau at Carter's Brook / 52
The Brim of the Well / 53
Coming Back / 57
Waking / 58
Day Without Omens / 59
The Bread Hot From the Oven / 60
A Sleeping Man Curses the Summer / 61
The Onion / 62

II / Stilt Jack

Author's Note: Ghazals / 67

(Thirty-eight untitled poems)
69-106

INTRODUCTION

Remembering John Thompson

The first time I met John Thompson, I was outraged. In the winter of 1974, a year after we had published his first book, *At the Edge of the Chopping There Are No Secrets*, House of Anansi Press had flown the poet to Toronto for a small party. We could scarcely wait to meet the man responsible for so many insightful letters, such radiant, passionate poetry. There John sat, his back squared against the wall, tense and surly, a much smaller, grimmer man than the woodsman-hero who welcomed us into the open spaces on his back-cover photo. He gave short shrift to our polite questions, and began to bark out insults into the embarrassed silence about mean publishers and a gutless Toronto literati that did not understand or value poetry. After less than an hour of this, the guests began to slip away.

The next day, I got another version; a lively, vigorous intelligence, a wry Lancashire humour, a firm integrity, and a breathtaking knowledge of world poetry: Neruda, Roethke, Lorca, Trakl, Yeats. Animatedly, Thompson talked of his life in the British army, of graduate school in the States, of teaching at Mount Allison University and the Dorchester Penitentiary where he had made the prisoners analyse Satan in *Paradise Lost* with touching results. By daylight, he looked hale and ruddy as he explained the appeal of rock-climbing and spelunking, the exploration of caves; later I heard that he was all but a professional in these hard, demanding sports.

Then that night, bottle of Jack Daniels at hand, he turned on me. He took a hunting knife from his khaki jacket, dropped it like a stone on the table, and asked if I had ever seen blood drawn. I couldn't read the voice or the smile, and simply ducked this challenge, or threat, or whatever it was. I know now that John was fascinated with any kind of gear — fishing tackle, rifles, mountaineering axes — and possibly he was showing off a good steel blade. Still, like any member of the gutless Toronto literati, I took my leave, wondering about Jekyll and Hyde, about the conflict of selves in the creative personality. It did not occur to me to think about alcohol. This was an era when a drink meant hard liquor, and almost everybody I knew drank like there was no tomorrow.

I remembered how dazzled I had been, when, shortly after coming to Anansi, I had read John's manuscript. It was lying there without fanfare on the slush-pile with the others. I picked it up, scanned a few poems, thinking not bad for nature poetry, and then hit:

Cauldron of leaves,
the sun a deadly furnace
under the branches . . .

This fierce image moves to a snapshot of the tree in winter, a "charred dancer" against the snow, then goes on to brood about what humans must settle for as a harvest: "the impure, the broken/green." I turned to the one about the crow and rabbit as a mystic design; then the long winter poem about the wind as "a white spice,/cure" and the trout perfect below the ice; I read "Partridge" and its terrifying lines about the juice of fear and death's thicket, and then the bird blazing forth at the end, strutting proudly among the world's decay.

Yes, nature poetry, but nature seen with a vengeance, as in Gerard Manley Hopkins, Dylan Thomas, or Ted Hughes (a favourite of John's; he re-read *Crow* like scripture), nature revealed in concentrated images that bring us close to painful cycles of death and regeneration, a world charged with grandeur where language and emotion count and where everything is at stake. Thompson's first critics were quick to praise his gift for capturing the New Brunswick environment, and, to be sure, his snowfields, birds, horse chestnuts, smithies, barns, and woodsmoke fairly rise up from the page. But there is more than landscape painting here: a horse is seen, great hooves sunk in red mud, and his anguish is shown to be our own, as we "relearn our balance,/reach out in the dark to test/ our crooked new bones."

Such breadth of vision and control of the language had been hard-won. John was born in 1938 into a British working-class family, and had grown up without material advantages. His father died when he was two, and his mother, employed as a mill-hand, put in long, hard hours away from home, ultimately bettering herself to become a bookkeeper. For her convenience, the boy was sent to live with relatives, a move he was bitterly to resent throughout his life. In a very real sense, he never went home again. Obviously bright, he got into Manchester Grammar School at the age of five — for his entrance, he wrote out the Lord's Prayer — where he impressed the teachers and went on to a BA in Honours Psychology at the University of Sheffield. Still in his teens, he next did his two years' mandatory service in the British Army, stationed in Germany in the mid-50s, where he began to write to pass the time.

I used to think John romanticized his army days: good comrades, up-the-establishment wit, and barroom fights; now I see that the military also met a need for structure, a longing for an everyday order to things, which is there in all the poems. How he got from the army to East Lansing, Michigan, in 1960 is not quite clear to me. A. J. M. Smith, the Canadian poet and anthologist, taught at Michigan State University, and perhaps John had sent him some of his work for judgement. At any rate he always felt that Arthur Smith had opened up the world of books to him, and wrote his PhD thesis in Comparative Literature under Smith, on French surrealism, including translations of the poet René Char. Smith also sparked in John an interest in Canada, and in 1966, with his American wife and daughter, Thompson moved to New Brunswick, to a farmhouse on the edge of the Tantramar, a haunting stretch of marsh and wilderness near the Bay of Fundy, celebrated in Canadian poetry since Bliss Carman and Charles G. D. Roberts.

Here he taught at Mount Allison University in Sackville, and wrote, and published poetry in the little magazines, as well as a cycle of translations from the Québécois poet Roland Giguère. This activity of translating and thinking about the language of poetry strongly affected his own work. For one thing, it gave him practice. But also, he became thoroughly grounded in poetic theory, especially European post-war surrealism, with its emphasis on the ideal image which should contain wordless power and universal resonance; on the miraculous qualities in daily things which the poet reveals by stripping away language, by recreating language afresh. At the edge of the chopping there are no secrets. Part of Thompson's achievement was to bring continental aesthetics to Canadian material, in a country where taking artistic theory too seriously can be viewed as weak, somehow colonial.

In the early 1970s, writing well, Thompson was popular with his students and devoted to his Tantramar farmhouse with its spectacular views, a storehouse of powerful images. Yet living in isolation seems to have offered too much time for drinking, for dark introspection, for family tensions and quarrels. At length, his wife and daughter moved back to the States; divorce proceedings began; rationally it seemed for the best. These things happened: *Chopping* was published; a handful of mixed, not always penetrating reviews; modest sales; no prizes. This is the fate of most first poetry books, but

John was quite angry about it. However, since *Chopping* he had been busy writing other poems, based on the ghazal, a Persian form. With a sabbatical and a grant, he came to Toronto to work on poetry and a book about René Char, and I saw him a fair amount then. Often we had good talks. Sometimes he was mean drunk.

During this period, I watched perhaps John's closest personal relationship, one that had given him support and encouragement for years, begin to erode, as it became clear that he was not just a heavy-drinking writer, but was alarmingly ill, an alcoholic. And it got much worse when, in the summer of 1975, he heard that his farmhouse in the Tantramar had burned down. His furniture, his sporting gear, his books, his very structure, all had gone up in flames, the loss to be a recurrent theme in *Stilt Jack*. His drinking went reeling out of control, and he returned to New Brunswick in desperate shape. Even his teaching was affected. His friends were sorely tried. A local doctor, consulted for a cure, told him he had never seen a man so mentally, emotionally, and physically destitute.

By nature proud and exacting, Thompson hated his affliction. All along there had been a valiant battle with drying out, with pills, with beer only, with just wine at dinner; but then, again, the fall from grace, the morning after, the self-disgust. Now, determined to stay sober and finish his second book, John moved to an apartment in Sackville and tried to assemble the best of his newer poems. Traditionally a ghazal is an erotic lyric, with a set number of verses and a recurrent rhyme; John had been experimenting with its possibilities for years. Typically he had first thrown the form to me as a challenge: I didn't even know what a ghazal was, did I? With some notion about African antelope, I confessed, no. Just as well, he said, because Anansi wasn't going to get the poems anyway. He'd go to a big publisher, Faber and Faber, somebody in New York, and what did I think about that?

Despite this manifesto, through that winter of 1975-76 the phone would ring late at night, and it would be John, slurring his words, begging me to approve the latest ghazal; then the garbled reading over long-distance wires, the accusation of indifference, the plea for editorial help, the call to friendship, the insults, the alcoholic's maddening repertoire of taunts, and rages, and gnawing need. I said of course I wanted to read the new poems, and of course I did. In April, shortly after Easter, I heard that he had killed himself.

The cause was said to be a brutal mix of barbituates and liquor. He had been drinking after a dry spell, it was late, and he had just completed a major work, a bad time for writers. There is evidence that he tried to shout down the heating register for help near the end. He had left a will in the apartment, written in ink on heavy parchment paper in his concise and distinctive hand, its legal ambiguities to cause a two-year delay in *Stilt Jack*'s publication. The poems had been given earlier to his friend, the poet Douglas Lochhead, who mailed the manuscript to Anansi, along with John's precise instructions on how it was to be published: the arrangement on the page, the order. About his art he was always careful.

When *Stilt Jack* arrived, I realized there were thirty-eight ghazals — John was exactly thirty-eight years old — and many lines that seemed to announce self-annihilation. Stunned by the bad news, I could hardly see the book as anything but a brilliant suicide note (although legally, his death was declared an accident), and certainly the anguish is there, from the very first lines:

Now you have burned your books; you'll go
With nothing but your blind, stupefied heart.

The cycle is, much of it, a night journey through a disordered personal cosmos. Instead of the healing clarity of the first book, we are plunged into chaos and old night: fish writhe with terror, women and God threaten or abandon, the very landscape buckles, and there is no bounty now in the everyday. We are fed "Crazy squash, burnt tomatoes, char of poems, sour milk" instead of *Chopping*'s redemptive onions and bread. Literary references (note Char/char), history, and pop culture (Janis Joplin) yammer insistently in the dark: "Yeats. Yeats. Yeats. Yeats. Yeats. Yeats. Yeats./Why won't the man shut up?" *Stilt Jack* brings us an inversion of the world shown in *Chopping*, an anti-*Chopping*. It's also a harder book to read, staccato with literary echoes, images stripped to the bone, a sputtering beat, arcana: the title alludes to a fish (John said), but also to a character in Yeats (Malachi Stilt-Jack), and a man on stilts.

The form is, yes, the ghazal, chosen, Thompson tells us, for its ability to present "contrasts, dreams, astonishing leaps." Whatever the ghazal may do for Persian poetry, the tight almost-couplets seem to me to rope in the avalanche here, and ride herd on chaos as the poet's entire life is assailed and found wanting: "I'm in touch with the gods I've invented:/Lord, save me from them." The vision is uncompromising:

I won't scream when I die:
I've burned everything;

words swarm on the back of my hand.
I don't run,

thick with honey
and sweet death

And yet, despite such horrors, after fifteen years I find I'm amazed at how positive the book can be, how serene. Even in hell, the poet is alive to physical presence, the "steam/from cows dreaming in frost," hardwood, pheasants, moons, "Dark April, black water, cold wind,/ cold blood on a hook." He revels in his craft, even while nagging at the apparent uselessness of poetry and the word. There's a Miltonic catalogue of flowers, New Brunswick-style (bellflower, mustard, swamp iris), and a Keatsian relish to "juices of clams/oysters, raw onions, moose heart and black olives." Thompson is exuberant, celebrating the world even as he implacably dispenses with it.

There is music, love:

A woman to quench the fires of my eye:
song: sweet, comely song.

He dances, though grieving, her hair tenting his body, hymns are sung, and a day of rejoicing is declared among the ruins.

At the end, in poem XXXVII, the heart shines forth without adjectives, no longer "blind and stupefied." The poet feels himself aware and waiting, cleansed. In the final ghazal, there is a friend. There is survival. There is language.

I'm still here like the sky
and the stove.

Can't believe it, knowing nothing
Friends: these words for you.

These beautiful, simple lines bring the cycle to rest after a much-troubled journey, and I'm thankful that John got to that place. The exact circumstances of his passing seem to make little difference now. Still, I have to wonder, more than fifteen years after his death, where he would have gone from there. Who can resist that sense of being somehow cheated by the gifted poet who dies too young or who self-destructs?

I wanted more books from John Thompson. The poems he agonized so obsessively over have not only outlasted those bleak days, but seem to have prevailed: "Friends: these words for you." Thompson always had a core group of loyal readers, and his audience has steadily grown over the years since 1976, even as poetry becomes, we are told, less sought after, unprized. He is still here. Like the sky, the stove. And with his books now available in a combined edition, where new readers will discover for themselves these words he left for us.

JAMES POLK/TORONTO

I

At the Edge of the Chopping
There Are No Secrects

for Meredith

WIFE

Your hands peeling and
        kneading the dough:

the work comes
        up from the thighs

and hips, through
        the leaned shoulders,

sweet drive of arms
        striking

down through the tough roots
        of the fingers;

in the dark
        of the oven

a moon gleams
        and fattens:

our winter bread,

        your shadow
huge on the wall.

HOUSEHOLD

bread: a silence; stillness before waking; honeycomb of sleep; wood in the heart of its seasoning; the long reach of the forest floating away into the half-light; I catch your odour out of the eye of my dream;

wine: a green-winged teal fast and sharp under the mist, dipping low into the canal; sheaves of early sun on the snow, lucent blue in the folds of drifts; tide at the full, muddied orange; I go down on my knees before your rich bitterness;

salt: a surprising red-hooded bird brings the winter tree into being: its shrivelled black apples suddenly discover themselves; you have awakened in all your bodies, your sharp cry pulls me up into the light.

PARTRIDGE

Stopping dead still
        on the road,
a trace of it
        sleeps in the air

(far back in the fir
        a faint rustle)

song:

coiled in spruce bark
an odour:
        buck heat or
the juice of fear;

loving a woman, I know
        death's thicket,

the must of rotting
        crab apples
in an abandoned orchard,

        this partridge
                strutting
through the dying fruit.

OUR ARCS TOUCH

If our arcs touch
it must be

as the taut snow setting
steel; steel
grass blade; death

we won't speak of

our folly,
    so cold, we can

bury these bones:

                  things
rise, the warmth:
so cold

our arcs touch,

it must be.

APPLE TREE

Cauldron of leaves,
the sun a deadly furnace
under the branches;

I cannot contain this summer
nor the charred dancer
exhausted
on the snow:

a head of burnt hair
crackling faintly,
the thin smoke
where a crow drifts
toward no home;

to be possessed or
abandoned by a god
is not in the language,

only the impure, the broken
green, the half-
formed fruit
we reach for in desire,

calling it
our harvest.

HORSE CHESTNUTS

I drive through
    with a clean nail:
        it goes

easy and true through the heart,
    but only with force
        through the tough

undershell, breaking out
    in a jagged, stiff,
        brown flower, crumbs

of yellow flesh spilling;

in the heel of my palm
    the sharp bite
        of the nail-head,

as I thread these fruits on a string
    to hang up in the sun.

FISH

a hammer perfectly steel, perfectly
struck

releases it, sweetly, to
rise

live through light water to
strike

what sleeps in a net of steel, blue
sun,

what might have been, wings and sure
release from,

but brings lost taste to metal,
blood,

and a hammer perfectly steel, perfectly
strikes,

what comes to light, live, sun, steel,
deep, from,

stone

HORSE

Your great hooves sunk
    in red mud, massive,
        still, you stare out

over the edge of the world;
    small fires
        flare in your eyes;

the sun turns in hunger
    about your dark head,
        sniffing the earth in you,
tasting your smoke,

and waits for your thighs
    to shift, your hooves
        to strain from the ground,

for some speech from your black muscles:

so the earth would tilt
    under your weight,

hawks plummet upward, the dead
    float in the air like flies,

and we, thrown from our warm furrows,
    relearn our balance,
        reach out in the dark to test

our crooked new bones.

BARN

Lightning struck her
but she didn't burn;
she fed five generations;

the ground's still hers
(they had to tear her down
shingle by shingle)
the green air;

in the muck I'll grow
crazy squash, cucumbers,

dance on my new horizon, watched
by her starry animals.

SCENE

The air warm with filth,
    animal hair, green wood
smoke,

a dimming yellow
    lamp-glow, gathering in

the horizon its
    dainty ships

        gleam of slight
coppery spires,

    a snowy trunk,

this squat boy peeing, quick, back of
    the shed, and

the thock of wood clean-
    split, the blade's
glitter

    just

by the door.

BLACK SMITH SHOP

The sun lights blue fires in the black stubble
on this face —
a shapeless rock
my words break on
as his laughter
breaks against the sun;

he has no words but this laughter,
and sounds, loud, crazy,
marrowy sounds which break
chunks out of the light;

but in his shop, in the intense
anthracite light,
not laughter, only

this rhythm of grunts, the face
icy with sweat, moving
with black grace around the horse,

paring crescents of horn from the hooves,
and this moaning speech he must draw,
as he sinks into his labour,

from the flesh of these bodies,
his shining beasts.

Outside again, I break open and shout,
shout,
and my sound comes back to me,

furry, alien, shining,
from the horn of the new moon,
out of this new dark.

TURNIP FIELD

Salt comes in with the wind
off the bay: some days
the air
       is thick with it; it stirs
the roots of the tongue, unearths
and splits the husks of taste —
balsam, marsh-hay, bull-flanks,
       berries, greens

which fuel this green fire,
this burning off
       of the dead hair

of turnips, big as heads,
piled up on the track: meat
for swine and cattle,

plucked junk earth eyes staring
at the man in blue overalls
whose honed fork glitters
in the flame as it
turns the smouldering leaves and stalks,
his mouth full of smoke

so he doesn't taste
fir, grass, muscle, apple,
the wind thick with salt,
but only watches
the way it stirs and
whips up his fires.

AFTER THE RAIN

After the rain, dead
still; not even a crow
menaces;

a hole opens in
the ground of grey cloud:

the wind
must unfold a night
in this hour of dawn.

COLVILLE'S CROW

This is the kind of bird
    will glide into your dreams fluttering
        like a leafy heart —

is this the crow you kept,
    like a weird machine,
        in your refrigerator,

to piece out
    the mechanics of the dark?

CROW AND RABBIT

A crow perching
    on the burst body
of a rabbit,

    shifting
the bones;

itself suddenly
    stilled, aged,
a construction of grey sticks,

giving up dead
    splinter after splinter
to the wind,

but staying as
    the rabbit bones stay,
marking a design on the road.

CROW'S WING

To lie close, to keep
    hold
of what you have made,
    your own;

cut fir, the green
    gone out of it,
is light, has
the touch of dust on it,

dust the hand taking
    the stain of plant,
weed, soil,
    stays free of in
the work;

a crow's wing nailed
    to the barn side dreams
dark flights,

but the hand keeps, silky,
    to the air,
  sure
of its blood-filled quarrels.

THE IMAGE

A dark flash:
black wings
    on white rock;

now the sun has burned off
    that image
the eye cannot hold;

but the darkness of the bird
still falls,
    swift,
  huge-shadowed

toward eyes holding now
the shining of a river,
    the fatness
  of an animal.

FIRST DAY OF WINTER

I step out into the air, it is almost
            blue, the cold
folds round my wrists;

crusty scabs on grey
            maple trunks, the last
faded gold tamarack needles.

ZERO

Cold, cold: iron
    blooms on my thighs; I strain
under ground, breaking
    through frozen earth —

then, bang my head,
    viciously, hours,
against the great barn doors, until

fires
crackle in every shingle,

and the huge black roof
    bursts up
a terrified bird,

beats painfully up meadow,
    and crashes

into the frozen hackmatack.

COLD WIND

In this country,
the wind kills
with swift birds
like bronze javelins;

they say, don't
mistake its images,
learn the beat of its cold wings,
the strain of its sinews
gathering on the haft;

and then they tell
of those who got the music
into their marrow:
the old men
who outdid its terror,
beating their tongues like oak leaves
against its fierce metal,

men with the straight eye,
insomniac,
the stubborn song
fast in the bone.

THE GREAT BEAR

You are standing here though you are gone
a thousand miles:

the green world shines, an apple deep
under ice;

I reach out
to stroke the muzzle of the Great Bear, glittering,
dipped, rooting for berries
under the snow in the next meadow.

JANUARY FEBRUARY MARCH ET CETERA

Your waist is growing lean, your skirt
    slops around your belly:
        you are proud;

you pick over crazy salads and feed me
    salt fish pie
        day after day;

god damn this winter when the air
    and women get thin
        and cold!

Building a fierce fire
    in the furnace, I imagine
        August —

bottles of thick Italian wine,
    huge milky potatoes bursting
        from the moist earth.

THE SUPERMARKET INVADED

Lit by the cold
our hungers ride from us,
slovenly beasts,

lope and crackle townwards,
overtaking scared automobiles,
drifting a strange scent
across recoiling thresholds;

inside, they sprawl, gorged,
in apple pulp and the sticky
juice of oranges, sleepily
gnawing marrow bones
and trembling beef hearts;

policemen weep, old ladies
in queer dancing shoes
giggle and shine; children
bang violently on the glass;

while the lord and master of foods,
hysterically red and white,
gobbles bad cheques, bangs
a mad music on the cash register,
and dreams of being easy with women,
learning to drink, and giving
credit unlimited.

DUNG DAY

Flies wake to sip balm, horses
    stare at the new sun;
the dark sinks with the old snow,
and in the alders, partridge bones
    surface;

and you, sluffing through the cold rows,
    pulling young onions;

nothing can be made of time
    or night, but feeling
roots fatten
    in the earth,
smelling moist dung:

a cure for disaster,
white morning
    in this kitchen of dead moons.

WHAT ARE YOU ASKING FOR?

What are you asking for?
I give nothing.

Feel, how the light strikes,
    an axe-blade,
across your hand,

and the snow
    cakes on your body:
mud on a sow's belly.

What are you asking for?

You have carried this in your arms
    for hundreds of years,
weightless.

I give nothing.

RETURN

Asleep or on the move where
the land is gone, curved
away, leaving you
blind;

those braille photographs you finger —
the shape: have you
got it?

This is only still
life: close
your ear to the dusty
skin of the city;
listen:

a hunting wing, a form
pressed in the rock,

from the woods where your shadow
glides, the cry
of old blood;

asleep or on the move it's gone
from you with the land curving
down to the cold:

it is time you set out.

"WINTER IS BY FAR THE OLDEST SEASON"
— *G. Bachelard*

Sweet sleep.
I would follow them out of this world
unmarked:

the meadow's snow, undulant,
the woods' cold,

as an animal grazing treads
into the sun and is slowly
burned from the field's edge.

* * *

With dark comes a fear of horses
and the smell of something moving
in back, always in cover, quick
between the shadows;

the sun is out of reach:
against the light I'd raise
earth, stone.

* * *

Deer
gone behind days of snow;

through the crook of your arm
I catch the moon
broken with frost;

in shadow
bones persist.

* * *

Snouts nuzzle the door
night hungry,

quick with our small salt
the table breathes,

we divide cold bread,
sip whiskey chilled in the snow:

the wind a white spice,
cure.

* * *

Sweet sleep:

the taste of war
and ripeness, smoke
coiling from bones;

to this cold we are
peculiarly knitted:

bitter apples and
crossed blood;

a bucket bangs
on a hackmatack post,

deep below the ice the trout
are perfect.

THE SKINS OF A DREAM

Paper birch, way back in the woods,
    whose barks
        curl back like the creamy

skins of a dream, whose whiteness
    curves as the arch
        of this woman's back, swaying,

intent, over the steaming pig's head,
    probing the rind's tenderness
        with a straw,

as the red arc of this windfall apple
    broken by a grey slug sleeping
        in wine, and

way back the woods are wine-dark,
    dark, unfolding
        roots, great stones, bread,

silences,
asking everything.

DOWN BELOW
for Roy Snowdon

At the edge of the chopping there are no secrets:

I am a trout, fat, come out
from under the bank, to lie
in the sun's mouth,
               in mid-stream,

a black fly stilled
    by the quiet, the clean
light, sealed
    in a bead of resin,

a deer's eye resting on white stone;

squatting, at ease with our sweat, smoking,
    there is nothing to say:
one maple shoot, green
    beyond green
is wife to us, we feed
    on roots;

desire and risk sleep, as though
    a candle burned
        far away
by our beds and fires.

THE NARROW ROAD

The snowfield rides away and
away, dreaming
of the lips of heaven:
white field bruised with warmth;

geese cry; I wake with them
on the narrow road, dawn
greens new shoots, ice turns milk;

the sweet way riding
beyond this familiar cold sleep.

There is a certain hour to move
without looking (I can almost touch
the end of all trees) to ride
white limits, meet unseen lips:

the great flocks rise to the light.

I like the snow blowing on the floor, things
that enter, rooms where
birds home and sing
as the wind rises, wings
lamping the branches of sleep; I need
no guide but these, and the oil
of woollen socks, and wine;

no goddess whitens my bed;
I am content
to reach into the still cold, without dreams,
listening to the voices fading
on the narrow road.

MOVING OUT, MOVING IN
for R.G.E.

The beauty of dumb animals
long silence
grows on the walls of our house;
the frost imagines our windows;

our water surrounds us with cold voices
of fish and mud;

the woods and
flies, coons, rats draw
our heat into their dark.

* * *

This is our misfortune
and maybe
our small grace:

we throw words at the dark
and the dark comes
back to us; a bird
is still for a moment
in our garden.

O we are muscular at our
tables, in our beds,
cowards under the moon.

* * *

I know you won't believe this, we are
so obstinate,
don't care for voices,

but after all, the poet names, almost
without speech:

because you are and said so,
we are:

you have opened the windows, the doors,
let in our animals, our sea, our woods;

with you, we inhabit our house,
move out and
let others move in.

BURNT COAT HEAD

We walk without
danger and move

full as the light, a body
without dress, limits,

that sweet
step of the new
foot feeling though
leaf, bark, fibre, and down

now the sap and all green flows
back in sleep, full

light: thus the meadow rises,
greens, dips, shines, steeps from us
into the sea, black;

I know you are here and
speak and the light through you

a meadow, clear green
of light, not calling, the open
shine, sown

with white birds: and above,
above these new birds,

that gathering
of the sun in two eyes

of a cross, killed hawks pointing

the meadow falling
to the sea black

the fierce shadows pressing the sun down
rising full, black on this

gallows, two hawks
claiming our day.

PICASSO: *LA JEUNE FILLE SUR LA BOULE;*
LASCAUX: *STAG FRIEZE*

A pale white horse crops the sky,
              a slender girl
                            arms curved up
into the clouds
              stands on the world;

something she does not notice
              is caught
                            between her hands,

her body light blue,
              something

caught between her hands:
a child's head, a bowl of apples, a flake
              of the sun,

and the sun through my window tangles
              in the charred antlers
                      of five deer
crossing a river under the earth:

the human will not hide its face
              behind the mist.

NORMAN TOWER'S

It's in winter I hear you, breathing
    under the snow, weeping
behind a wall of frost.

I don't know whether you are calling me,
    or the team,
long dead, from the barn.

Is it weeping?

On a clean birch hook, the harness
    hangs stiff, so old
the wind can't shift it.

In the half morning, a single gunshot —
    no one hears; the deer
lie warm and still in their yards.

Weeping behind a wall of frost, under the snow
    frozen beets, maybe

your breathing.

ON THE TOLAR CANAL

I know the brant are wheeling in great flocks in the black rain
over the Jolicure Lakes,
and on the High Marsh Road an old barn, almost the last,
is burning;

I have been watching for hours by the canal, wrists
cold as spent shotgun shells;

water and reeds;

in the last light a new tin barn roof lifts and
cuts like a goose wing: I shoot
and the roof shouts and sinks;

(I have seen men gun so hard their eyes
blacken, their foreheads crack, seamed with frost)

I am half-way back, climbing over a dyke which is
beginning to float:
a man is talking to me in a strange language, or is it
the thin blade of this dyking spade, newly oiled, that speaks?

He is asking why I have murdered and buried his ancestors.

THE CHANGE

It's in the dark we approach
    our energies, that instant
the tide is all fury, still,
    at the full:

as that time I lost an axe-blade
    in the chopping,
and listened, for days, to the rust
    gathering; and that night

I didn't find it, but came upon
    a cow moose blind, stinking
with heat, moaning, and

hooving the black peat with
    such blood, such fury,
the woods broke open, the earth

    recovered her children,
her silences, her poems.

EWE'S SKULL ON THE ABOIDEAU AT CARTER'S BROOK

Every day I cross the aboideau it's there,
    shifted, less bloody, cleaner, strangely
untouched by dust. As I pass

it seems to rock, gently, in
    a satisfying, crushed sleep, nourishing
the iron blow across the nose.

I wonder why you aren't pure: your pole-axe each time
    in marriage with the bone, your feeding
on blood they, twitching, sleep away;

and the meat, hung, clean from your knife,
    the sweet gods of your barn.

Every day on the aboideau, this ewe's skull,
    bloody, clean:

between these two waters: the salt scummed
    with ice, thick with sea-mud, the fresh,
clear with the iron of the woods,

    under your sign, your bone,
I make my peace.

THE BRIM OF THE WELL

In nests we live on heat,
    small bread, worms:

an arm not lifted against the wind;

    winter on dead twigs, broken grass,
women in small beds, thick
    with cloth, dry;

  rust talk, shrunk fruit;
    seek

    the cold, the wind wrapping
the bone, zero, here

    snow laps the plain, grows
on the spruce wall:
    fruit for children,
for the heart, glittering
    on a stump, a tried blade;

face frost, sniff space, ice,
    for its salt, its soil:

lie with the crow on the dump,
    pass through the wall of his eye:
what brightness of flesh he probes,
    what shadows,
the lip of a wound;

whose children are we? We have
    mistaken home.

* * *

Free of the warmth, outside, something
        happens:
sea hammering softly on a dyke, shingles
        soaked black by rain, smell
of old wood —
        cedar, wings
                beating,
refusing, earth
knowing itself, scenting
        its prey, its grave;

the poem a sheet of blue steel
        hammering
the meadow, fierce

in the air, shreds
        of beaten fruit,
        a bone
from before time, the earth's under
        a curving weave, comb

of a mad cock flaming
        at dawn,
                blood
of a maple split
        by frost,
                lightning, death's
acreage.

* * *

Not one grain of rust sleeps
on my fury: I insist
    on my wounds, my death:

clean axe
        in new wood

I spring juice.

* * *

Trees sweet with the bodies
    of women clean
to the wind,

green wood burning
    to coals, sap hiss.

* * *

I raise my red arm against the wall of the woods:
        salute,
it is eaten
into flashes of snow, catspruce needles, shreds
of faintly flapping birchbark,

a black root full of sound,

coldbroken, earthed, I lie you
lie
    would the earth come back to us
not on her breasts
    if the earth came back to us
not on her warm belly
    when the earth comes back to us
apples black stars broken gardens

on her cold thighs
    half buried
in frozen peat.

COMING BACK

Night is day, winter a single
    gust of wind which bangs
        the moon;

the time it takes
    to lift my hand to grasp
        the smell of balsam

I break the buried rock
    of an immense journey

and stand before the window
    my eyes rimy
        with frost, glittering
with owls' flights, my mouth
    full of dead ferns;

around my wife's hand swirls
    a mist of flour,
the hands of my daughter
    gleam with paint,

and I come, simply, bringing
    a few fir cones
which have lain for months
    under the snow,

back to the quiet, knowing
    those terrible iron tongues
no longer hammer
    against the walls of my house.

WAKING

As you wake, watch
    the leaves and branches pull

softly from your flesh and slide
    to the bright window,

your black pig
    and bat shapes

float down into your bones;

raise both your hands
    into the air, and spread

the fingers: see
    how they flutter

from deep within, insanely,
    as the sun strips off

layer after layer of dark feathers,
    the light cutting your body

from the shadows which grow
    from lying down close to yourself.

DAY WITHOUT OMENS

It is that hour when winter, a knife
clean
as the salt wind
probes those wounds we no longer disguise,

lays against the bone its cold voice;

it is a woman suddenly
called back into all her body;

a green branch, this candle,
heedless, still
under our roof;

we resist mystery, the smoke
of old fires:

in the waking of our marrow, now
the call
of the first bird,

the breath of our white voices.

THE BREAD HOT FROM THE OVEN

Under the ice with its bouldery death's faces
hidden forms begin to churn the tides,
a wink of blood starts the moon's white track,
fish rise
to their eternal lives;

this morning the bread hot from the oven
sounds with voices:
terrible blows struck
below an unimaginable prairie;

deer break from a mesh of dreams
and two bears burn with the dawn,
cursing the earth's white face
in a stony blood dance
that I feel as words I do not know,
of immense weight,
that I would carry with me,
burdens, until

they appear as they are:
the gods of this place,
this household,
words so light, so still
they are heard only at night
when the earth moves
inwardly:

root songs, that our bodies wake
freighted with melancholy
and the joy of something
a moment held
in our empty hands.

A SLEEPING MAN CURSES THE SUMMER

Without darkness, with no
edge of things,

the sun whitening in an endless
green field,

udders huge — the fat
of all: sown
to sleep,

the orchard lunatic with apples.

Would the fox come
    from the drowse, the deer
quickening
quiver into the plains,

a flicker of night at midday,
    the silent frost
thinning the stars,

and the green withered
    to a dark edge, beyond which

the black: your real
    hands and eyes.

THE ONION

I have risen from your body
full of smoke, charred fibres;

the light kicks up off
the glazed snow: I have to
turn from its keenness,
its warmth, seeking
darkness, burying ground;

I am without grace, I cannot shape
those languages, the knots
of light and silence:
the newness of being
still, the press
of the snow's whiteness.

Young steers turned from the barn
stand, furry stones, streaked
with dung,
cold light, thin
February snow.

In this kitchen warmth I reach
for the bouquet
of thyme and sage, drifting
in the heat: a world crumbles
over my hands, I am washed
with essences;

I cup the onion I watched grow all summer:
cutting perfectly through its heart
it speaks a white core, pale

green underskin, the perfections
I have broken, that curing grace
my knife releases;

and then you are by me, unfolded
to a white stillness, remade warmth on warmth.

So we turn from our darkness,
our brokenness,
share this discovered root,
this one quiet bread
quick with light, thyme, that deep
speech of your hands which always
defeats me, calling me through strange earths
to this place suddenly yours.

II

Stilt Jack

*for my daughter,
and for S.*

Those great sea-horses bare their teeth and laugh at the dawn.
W. B. YEATS

May God preserve the sickness of my eye.
TRUMBULL STICKNEY

I have only to lift my eyes, to see the Heights of Abraham.

GHAZALS

Originating in Persia, the ghazal is the most popular of all the classical forms of Urdu poetry. Although the form as it is now written first appeared in Persia, it probably goes back to the 9th century. The great master of the ghazal in Persia was Hafiz (1320-1389). Five hundred years later, Ghalib, writing in Urdu, became an equally brilliant master of the form, which is full of conventions, required images, and predetermined postures.

The ghazal proceeds by couplets which (and here, perhaps, is the great interest in the form for Western writers) have no necessary logical, progressive, narrative, thematic (or whatever) connection. The ghazal is immediately distinguishable from the classical, architectural, rhetorically and logically shaped English sonnet.

The link between couplets (five to a poem) is a matter of tone, nuance: the poem has no palpable intention upon us. It breaks, has to be listened to as a song: its order is clandestine.

The ghazal has been practised in America (divested of formal and conventional obligations) by a number of poets, such as Adrienne Rich. My own interest in the 'form' lies in the freedom it allows — the escape, even, from brief lyric 'unity'. These are not, I think, surrealist, free-association poems. They are poems of careful construction; but of a construction permitting the greatest controlled imaginative progression.

There is, it seems to me, in the ghazal, something of the essence of poetry: not the relinquishing of the rational, not the abuse of order, not the destruction of form, not the praise of the private hallucination.

The ghazal allows the imagination to move by its own nature: discovering an alien design, illogical and without sense — a chart of the disorderly, against false reason and the tacking together of poor narratives. It is the poem of contrasts, dreams, astonishing leaps. The ghazal has been called 'drunken and amatory' and I think it is.

JOHN THOMPSON

I

Now you have burned your books: you'll go
with nothing but your blind, stupefied heart.

On the hook, big trout lie like stone:
terror, and they fiercely whip their heads, unmoved.

Kitchens, women and fire: can you
do without these, your blood in your mouth?

Rough wool, oil-tanned leather, prime northern goose down,
a hard, hard eye.

Think of your house: as you speak, it falls,
fond, foolish man. And your wife.

They call it the thing of things, essence
of essences: great northern snowy owl; whiteness.

II

In this place we might be happy; blue-
winged teal, blacks, bats, steam

from cows dreaming in frost.
Love, you ask too many questions.

Let's agree: we are whole: the house
rises: we fight; this is love

and old acquaintance.
Let's gather the stars; our fire

will contain us; two,
one.

III

It's late. Tu Fu can't help me. There's no wind.
My blue shirt hangs from the cuffs on the line.

I can't talk to God. Tonight, I dug
three hills of potatoes. Sadness, what's that?

Give up words: a good knife, honed; and a needle
drawn across an iron bar, set in a matchbox.

Damn these men who would do my work for me;
my tomatoes redden by the window.

All spring and summer (this inch,
these noosed three moons) I fished trout.

One line of poetry dogs me; the newspapers,
the crazy world.

I'm thinking of you. Nashe. Rats on my window sill.
The dirt under my fingernails.

Lord, lord. I'm thinking of you.
I'm gone.

IV

I fed my marrow with the juices of clams,
oysters, raw onions, moose heart and black olives:

a green crust, a man banging a raw
elbow-bone on my table, stopped me.

I thought all women were beautiful, and I was ready:
drunk, I'd lie with dark iron; sober, walk away.

There's a health will lead me to the grave, the worm;
resisting axioms, I'll dream,

lie down on my right side, left side, eat dung:
Isaiah greets me; he wants to talk; we'll feed.

V

Don't talk to me of trifles; I feel the dirt in these:
what brightens when the eye falls, goes cold.

I have so many empty beer bottles, I'll be rich:
I don't know what I'd rather be: the Great Bear, or stone.

I feel you rocking in the dark, dreaming also
of branches, birds, fire and green wood.

Sudden rain is sweet and cold. What darkens
those winds we don't understand?

Let's leave the earth to be; I'm asleep.
The slow sky shuts. Heaven goes on without us.

VI

My daydreams defeat me, and cigarettes;
in the cold I'm myself: two follies.

I want to cut myself off. Bone says:
I'll dance, and you with me.

Bats flit at close of eve; anger
dies with the wind; partridge roost.

The moon, the moon, the moon.
A pine box; Herodotus; no tears, a settling:

what lies in its right place, lives. Brothers,
sisters, true friends lie down in darkness.

Dreams and the cold: I'm drunk on these.
Sisters, brothers, fathers, friends, I don't forget.

VII

Terror, disaster, come to me from America.
Middle of the night. Highs in the seventies. Penny Lane. Albany.
                                          Albany?

What letters of van Gogh I remember, I've forgotten.
He cut off his ear. Crows. Potato eaters.

Crazy squash, burnt tomatoes, char of poems, sour milk,
a candle gone down: is this my table?

I'm waiting for Janis Joplin: why,
why is it so dark?

I talk to a poet: he goes on, drunk:
I pray he's writing, don't dare ask.

Hang on, hang on: I'm listening,
I'm listening to myself.

VIII

I forget: why are there broken birds
behind me; words, goddammit, words.

I want to wake up with God's shadow
across me: I'm a poet, not a fool.

Porcupine are slow, fast in their quills:
they'll come to your iron bar, believing themselves and apples.

I don't want to die bloody on the highway:
I travel back roads, the dirt;

don't complain about going: sometimes
think I'll never get to sleep.

Everything reminds me. I want to push.
Black spruce; strange fires.

Snow will come. Wind. A kind of age.
What's at my feet must move quickly.

October; 3 A.M.; I go out and take a rose,
and the sea, and thorns.

I want to give everything to this burnt flower: I've nothing;
I bury my face; set it in water.

IX

Yeats. Yeats. Yeats. Yeats. Yeats. Yeats. Yeats.
Why wouldn't the man shut up?

The word works me like a spike harrow:
by number nine maybe I get the point.

It's all in books, save the best part; God knows
where that is: I found it once, wasn't looking.

I've written all the poems already,
why should I write this one:

I'll read Keats and eye the weather too,
smoke cigarettes, watch Captain Kangaroo.

Big stones, men's hands, the shovel
pitched properly. The wall of walls rises.

If I weren't gone already, I'd lie down right now:
have you ever heard children's voices?

Sometimes I think the stars scrape at my door, wanting in:
I'm watching the hockey game.

Likely there's an answer: I'm waiting,
watching the stones.

X

A pineapple tree has grown in this kitchen
two years, on well water. Right here,

a man went to set a fire in the stove
and the blaze froze on the match.

Those winds: in summer turn the head rancid, in winter
drive a cold nail through the heart down to the hardwood floor.

Daisies, paintbrush, bellflower, mustard, swamp iris;
hackmatack, crowns driven northeast: they're there.

Pigs fattened on boiled potatoes; horses mooning in hay;
in the woodshed he blew his head off with a shotgun.

XI

The fox is quick; I haven't seen him; he's quick.
The rainbow strikes one foot at my door.

The kettle lid lifts: must be fire,
it keeps.

It's too dry to plough; gulls grow in the cut corn,
owls, harriers: so many swift wings.

There's all the noise here,
it's so quiet:

the sky sleeps on the backs of cattle,
streams slow to black.

Last night I died: a tired flie woke me.
On White Salt Mountain I heard a phrase carving the world.

XII

after Tu Fu

I'm here at last, love this bed:
we stay up at night talking the moon down.

A bad mistake: looking for new flowers,
finding frost.

We'll fish tommy cod: that's enough;
come April I know where to go.

If the man gives me enough pennies
I'll go across the marsh and buy a little field.

Why be my own Job's comforter?
A bottle of cheap rye: an empty head.

XIII

The rook-delighting heaven?
I've seen one crow.

The cock pheasant I'll nail: he's beautiful,
quick; I know the tree, the spot; He's disappeared.

They dragged him home behind the tractor:
fat beef; the dark wound in the loam.

I think we should step out the door:
they're calling: men, women and dead voles.

I wish there were less wine: I'd want more;
breasts, breasts.

I'm in touch with the gods I've invented:
Lord, save me from them.

XIV

All night the moon is a lamp on a post;
things move from hooks to beautiful bodies. Drunk.

I think I hear the sound of my own grief:
I'm wrong: just someone playing a piano; just.

Bread of heaven.
                In close.

In dark rooms I lose the sun:
what do I find?

Poetry: desire that remains desire. Love?
The poet: a cinder never quite burned out.

XV

If I give everything away
it's because I want to take everything;

catching things from the air, I'll force
a perfect flower from the blue snow;

I can look at the sun with open eyes,
the moon laughs in my kitchen;

I think of children and the unwise:
they have terrible strength;

when will you,
will you?

The drunk and the crazy live for ever,
lovers die:

our mouths are wet with blood:
is it the blood we'll live by?

If I give you my right arm,
will you

XVI

The barn roof bangs a tin wing in the wind;
I'm quite mad: never see the sun;

you like sad, sad songs that tell a story;
how far down on whiskey row am I?

I believe in unspoken words, unseen gods:
where will I prove those?

If I wash my hands will I disappear?
I'll suck oil from Tobin's steel and walnut.

If one more damn fool talks to me about
sweetness and light...

I'm looking for the darkest place;
then, only then, I'll raise my arm;

someone must have really socked it to you:
were the lips made to hold a pen or a kiss?

If there were enough women I wouldn't write poetry;
if there were enough poetry

XVII

I pick things out of the air: why not?
No one shall sleep.

Lift me up, lift me up…, he said:
I would have, I would.

I don't need Page's arm:
I've got fire: I'm laughing, laughing.

We've all been cold. I was born mad.
Wooden matches strike anywhere.

If there's joy for one day, there is, there is:
they that sow in teares: shall reap in joy.

Celebrate. Celebrate. Celebrate.
Death cannot celebrate thee.

One fish, one bird,
one woman, one word,

that does it for me, and the last word of *Ulysses* is
yes.

XVIII

A man dancing into life:
ashes to ashes; O my America.

Friends, I believe I'll burn first:
I'll find you by compass: dead reckoning.

Sing no sad songs. A tree stands:
lay a stone against it.

Cast a cold eye, cast
a cold eye:

when I meet you again I'll be all light,
all dark, all dark.

XIX

I try for oblivion, dirt
and a woman:

my right hand breaks;
new snow;

I drive into a strange heart, and lift
out of all this beauty something

myself, a fish hook tinged with blood,
a turned furrow,

potatoes, fish, those who love them,
must come.

XX

I begin again:
why should not young men be mad?

Trial of my own images, I dream
of one thing.

The curve of a line weaves
a celestial equator:

My child. The dark
horse in the rain.

Let Meton speak, but leave
the numbers lie as stones.

I pick over
last night's food.

Now let us servants rise like Atlantis.
By lying down, I'll wake, depart in peace.

The tide ebbs from my hand.
I want to join blood.

Loaves of bread remembered:
eat salt and tell the truth.

Grief the knife, joy
the vulnerable bread.

Eat, let the blade
be surprised by joy.

XXI

I know how small a poem can be:
the point on a fish hook;

women have one word or too many:
I watch the wind;

I'd like a kestrel's eye and know
how to hang on one thread of sky;

the sun burns up my book:
it must be all lies;

I'd rather be quiet, let the sun
and the animals do their work:

I might watch, might turn my back,
be a done beer can shining stupidly.

Let it be: the honed barb drowsing in iron water
will raise the great fish I'll ride

(dream upon dream, still the sun warms my ink
and the flies buzzing to life in my window)

to that heaven (absurd) sharp fish hook,
small poem, small offering.

XXII

I'm just a man who goes fishing:
if there's a woman with green eyes, there is.

My land's wet: I'll wait, perched on a post;
I know my seeds will alarm the sun.

Dark April, black water, cold wind,
cold blood on a hook.

I won't scream when I die:
I've burned everything;

words swarm on the back of my hand.
I don't run,

thick with honey
and sweet death

I love to watch the trout rising
as I fall, fall.

XXIII

What is it you want to say? Say it now.
I hear children; the fallow; pig's blood.

Churn, churn; all in black:
the milk I want, I want.

There must be an end:
flowers deceive me;

we are all poor, poor:
the cattle lift their huge eyes.

Where am I? Where are you?
The Lord stuck on a bulletin board.

Put two words together: likely
it's your name.

I don't know mine:
the words have taken it, or someone's hand.

I dream myself into being,
a poor man.

I'm a great fish, swallowing everything:
drunk all my own seas.

Say it now: honey from the sweet, drunk, dead:
I lift my eyes,

I'm listening; the moon sinks;
I chart the back of my hand.

I don't hear your words: I hear the wind,
my dreams, disasters, my own strange name.

XXIV

Always the light: a strange moon,
and the green I don't understand;

knives set in order; somewhere else,
eyes looking back across a terrible space:

a meeting in a garden, hands, knees, feet
in the dirt: animals; the flies feeding;

what comes from this? pour wine on it:
have you read all your blood?

No prophecy in the furrow: only the print of bare feet,
anxious for what grows;

nothing? one small leaf is a heart:
a leaf we divide, dividing us.

Lift up the soily stones,
feel the burn of lime,

a handful of seeds, a handful of earth,
silence in thunder on the tongue:

a long waiting without stars,
ending in snow.

XXV

In a dark wood,
and you in a strange bed.

In midsummer I dream great snows
and a man come to ask about fish.

Divinity sounds in machines,
shines darkly from the pleasure of birds.

What do I believe? I hear the crack
of corn fattening at night.

The blood at night sounds
with your swimming.

Where are all our books and stories?
I look into dark water:

we have been there: our eyes
join deep below the surface.

If I ask questions, you'll show me
some beautiful thing you have made.

XXVI

Surrounded by dirty glasses, nights
of love: the world is full of...

and then to be honest, as a hair,
a still hand, a plain box;

caught by bad music, strange meat,
the smell of old tin;

there are ways, and signs: the woods
point one way,

the words: there is a word:
there are words, lie about us,

dogs and the night and children
poured out in looseness

and children
on the grassy ground.

XXVII

You have forgotten your garden (she said)
how can you write poems?

That things go round and again go round.
In the middle of the journey...

Folly:
the wildflowers grow anyway.

I wait for a word, or the moon, or whatever,
an onion, a rhythm.

All the rivers look for me,
find me, find me.

The small stone in my hand weighs years:
it is dark.

To turn, and remember, that
is the fruit.

XXVIII

I learn by going;
there is a garden.

Things I root up from the dirt
I'm in love with.

First things: lost. The milky saucer,
of last things a siren.

Please, please be straight, strait,
stone, arrow, north needle.

I haven't got time for the pain,
name your name,

the white whale, STILT JACK, in her face,
where I have to go.

XXIX

The Lord giveth.
I wrote letters,

sealing,
stitches of emptiness.

Absence makes what?
Presence, presence.

Music, beautiful stories,
tin, tin cans,

fingers on a pine table,
fire.

Love, black horse, a turned
head, voice:

breaking my heart, laughing;
knife, fork and spoon,

turnips, stored words, rip-rap and all that
etcetera,

something
taken away.

XXX

The mind tethered, head
banged with a hardwood stick;

sense a mangled iron
and the fire gone cold.

Read it all backwards; start with Act III;
a clean pair of heels.

The muck of endings; drunk beginnings;
yattering histories, rodomontades, anabases.

Get to the bloody point:
seize the needle,

day, plainness: cold sea, that
one grain of sand.

XXXI

I'll wait; watch
Look, look.

Poor people. Poor
We're rich; beautiful.

Brant: the Great Missaquash Bog:
My love: a splash: safe.

I fire my right arm out strait.
My wife's sledgehammer; my woman's eye.

I'm not good enough.
Sufficient is Thine arm alone.

XXXII

A woman to quench the fires of my eye:
song: sweet, comely song.

We sing hymns: we care
for the sound of grief and the grieving.

But we'll dance, her ashen hair
tenting my body;

we join hands, eyes, lips: one:
as safe as a toad in God's pocket.

Love the final loss, the last
giving.

This is the day which the Lord hath made;
we will rejoice and be glad in it.

XXXIII

Dark as the grave. The deep lightning
whiteness of swans' wings.

I make necklaces for a woman and
my daughter: gentle harvests.

Anger dies with the wind. In near-sleep
I'm a salt-water trout spilling seed.

The want. The hunting harrier
bound to earth. The fox denned.

I go clothed like a bear: ride
against the sun. Then the snow sleep:

I have only to lift my eyes to see
the Heights of Abraham.

XXXIV

I surrender to poetry, sleep
with the cinders of Apollo.

Belay to words:
Stubai, Kernmantel, Bonnaiti,

Karrimor, K.2., Nanga Parbat,
Jumar, Eiger, Chouinard, Vasque.

Annapurna. The mountain wakens:
a closing hand.

Love lies with snow, passion
in the blue crevasse. Grief on summits.

Let me climb: I don't know to what:
north face, south face?

Maybe the roping down,
the last abseil.

XXXV

after Mir Taqi Mir

Love, look at my wounds, the shame I've drunk —
I wouldn't wish such suffering on my bitterest enemy.

Walk the graveyards: did you know the dead could have such
                                                                            hair?
But devouring fate would have gnawed at them forever.

You're well off: don't make your home with this history of
                                                                            disasters:
The cold desert always destroys my bed.

I know: your pale green eyes speak what's final:
Sweet deaths never spoken of, beautiful terrors.

It's clear: the broken moon is suddenly full for me.
As always, drops gather into a limitless ocean.

XXXVI

I don't know

Desire.
Taste of the sea: salt.

The scorch of letters written
from the poem's isolate place.

I feel all the weight:
have I dared the dark centre?

We'll rise as one body.
A wedge of geese.

Time: slow as rivers,
entering us as the wings of birds.

Soft now. The join deep as bone.
Safe as the unwounded sap.

When you look into my eyes,
The moon stills as a Kestrel.

We'll gather all our lives and deaths
In a lightning harvest.

XXXVII

Now you have burned your books, you'll go with nothing.
A heart.

The world is full of the grandeur,
and it is.

Perfection of tables: crooked grains;
and all this talk: this folly of tongues.

Too many stories: yes, and
high talk: the exact curve of the thing.

Sweetness and lies: the hook, grey deadly bait,
a wind and water to kill cedar, idle men, the innocent

not love, and hard eyes
over the cold,

not love (eyes, hands, hands, arm)
given, taken, to the marrow;

(the grand joke: *le mot juste:*
forget it; remember):

Waking is all: readiness:
you are watching;

I'll learn by going:
Sleave-silk flies; the kindly ones.

XXXVIII

Should it be passion or grief?
What do I know?

My friend gives me heat and a crazy mind.
I like those (and him).

Will it all come back to me?
Or just leave.

I swing a silver cross and a bear's tooth
in the wind (other friends, lovers, grieving and passionate).

I've looked long at shingles:
they've told.

I'm still here like the sky
and the stove.

Can't believe it, knowing nothing.
Friends: these words for you.